W9-BGI-561

The Lost Body of Childhood

Poems by

David Dayton

Copper Beech Press
Providence, Rhode Island
1979

Published by
Copper Beech Press
Box 1852 Brown University
Providence, RI 02912

Distributed by
The New York State Small Press Association
Box 1264 Radio City Station
New York, NY 10019

The author gratefully acknowledges the periodicals listed below, which first published some of this book's poems, several in earlier versions.

Big Moon	"Disrobing the Body of Thought"
	"Dreaming Back"
	"Song for Our Nights"
Grove	"The Life of Weeds"
Kayak	"Family"
	"Saying Good-bye to the Bureaucrats at the Museum of Hopelessness"
Marilyn	"On My Own"
Montana Gothic	"After Hearing Roethke Read"
New Letters	"Late Spring Night, Driving Home with Friends"
Poetry Northwest	"The Lost Body of Childhood"
	"The Precepts of the Obvious"
	"Wind and Strategy"
Puddingstone	"At the Laundromat"
Stinktree	"A Backslidden Preacher's Son, To His Mother"

The cover illustration is reproduced from a photograph by Jerry N. Uelsmann, and is used with his permission.

Library of Congress Cataloging in Publication Data

Dayton, David, 1952-
    The lost body of childhood.

    I. Title.
PS3554.A974L6   811'.5'4   79-16222
ISBN 0-914278-25-8

The symbol * indicates that a stanza has been interrupted for pagination.

Contents

I   Amazing Grace   *3*
A Backslidden Preacher's Son, To His Mother   *4*
Family   *6*
Song for Our Nights   *8*
At the Laundromat   *9*
The Precepts of the Obvious   *10*
Postcard from the Heartland   *11*
Apart   *12*
On My Own   *13*
Saying Good-bye to the Bureaucrats
    at the Museum of Hopelessness   *15*

II   Dreaming Back   *19*
My Brother's Face   *22*

III   Wind and Strategy   *31*
The Tie That, Binding, Liberates   *32*
Houseplants   *33*
The Life of Weeds   *34*
Strawberry   *35*
Eating a Peach   *36*
Another Portrait of the Artist   *38*
The Noble in Exile   *42*
Dusk   *44*
After Hearing Roethke Read   *45*
Disrobing the Body of Thought   *46*
Late Spring Night, Driving Home with Friends   *47*
Conversation with the Inner Man   *48*
The Mesmerist's Pearl   *50*
For a Child Dreaming   *51*
Blinking and Breathing   *52*
April Night, Turning In   *53*
Navigation Self-Taught   *54*
The Lost Body of Childhood   *55*

For Nancy

I

Amazing Grace

My father can't always hide his regret.
Though he smiles, I'll see his eyes wince
before they turn from what I've said.
He blames himself for changing too late,
wishes he'd never been the father
his father taught him to be, the household
Almighty. His short-fused wrath was
terrible to witness: an inflamed, yelling man
buffeting a cornered child. What hurt
him more than us was the discrepancy
between his rage and the face he put on
as reverend: meek, beaming to everyone.
In a dream when I was small I opened a door
and found my father as Christ suffering
on the cross. I cried bitterly for us both,
sons forsaken. Recently, this man
humbled himself on the phone, suggesting
my heresies took root in his doubts, that
my discontents grew from his complaints.
In a roundabout way I said: "Forgive yourself.
Or accept me as I am." I know he worries
about my soul. I've taken off the helmet
of salvation and seen my face as it was
before I was born. The church I attend
is small, moon-lit and full of echoes.
I have communion, but little fellowship.
Sometimes an errant tune recalls a hymn
and I'll find I still know entire stanzas.
I hear them sung, hear my father's voice
call on the congregation to bow their heads.

A Backslidden Preacher's Son, To His Mother

1.

We are in a theater,
facing a stucco wall with a small window,
its white curtains thrashing.
Magically lifted to its sill,
I see a sapling bowed to the ground,
and farther off, a black funnel cloud
whirling toward us.
I turn to tell you, but can't.
You're still in your seat,
knees crossed, arms hugging yourself,
waiting for the movie to begin.
I sit down and press into your sweater.
Dark in the scent of your perfume,
I take a final breath
and wait for the building to fall.

2.

In fever
I felt the cold, white palm
of God's angel,
heard your voice through the cloud of pain
explaining His plan,
the circle of divine reason.
What it encompassed,
that black hole in the middle of everything,
was faith.

3.

Mother, you know what you know,
a peace that surpasses understanding.
I study my dreams
like the oracles of some lost religion,
falling into faith
as in a dream when ground gives way
and you drop, tensed for the shock
that never comes.
Almost, I think,
kneeling on the bathroom floor,
I am almost there this time.
And like a feverish child,
I call out again the names of God.

Family

For the longest time
I must have felt it was all a mistake

What did I have to do with you
Who wore the parts of my face
Divided among yourselves
Like a shared joke

The morning I left
You gave me a gourd to wear around my neck
That shook with a clatter of seeds
Like your voices in argument

When people ask where I'm from
I trace my fingers over a map of air

There are days I'm sure
I forget you entirely

Then I'll find myself mouthing
One of the homilies you set the table with
Mother

Father
Of second thoughts
I have the acids of your stomach
Now and then that pain
Like a swift kick in the small of my back

Sometimes at night
Scouting the perimeters of grief
I think how hard it must be to watch grow
The ignorance you gave birth to
Having thought you knew the answers

Sisters
Brother
What do I know that I can tell you

In the deepest part of myself
Is a hieroglyph
I have only begun to decipher

Left there by some forgotten ancestor
Is it the emblem of love
Or death

You tell me

What secret
Makes us tremble like conspirators
Whenever we meet

Song for Our Nights

To Nancy

You arrived here after nearly twenty years
to throw your arm across my chest
like a life ring,
fingers curled loosely
where my neck and shoulder join.
With both hands bent around your arm,
I hang on,
buoyed by a sudden lightness.
Listening to your breath,
I begin to understand
what my father meant by "grace."
But I have no god to thank,
just you
beside me underneath this open window
and this breeze
that has come such a long way
to cool our skin.

At the Laundromat

Two housewives peel shirts and blouses
from a heap of tangled clothes.
They snap the wrinkles out
and smooth each garment on the table,
folding with a flurry of hands
deftly as bakers shaping dough.

The one about my mother's age
sings to herself,
just loud enough for us to hear,
''What a Friend We Have in Jesus.''

As you reach into the dryer,
I slap and grab your ass.
Your tits bounce up
when you wheel around to hug me
with underwear and damp socks.

I feel the women's eyes
appraising us with glances
I never turn in time to catch.
I guess they wonder if we're man and wife.

Compatriots, we face each other
holding the corners of our flowered sheet
and, stepping forward,
fold the flag of our country.

The Precepts of the Obvious

First you must understand that where you are going
Is not any place you have ever been.
Yes, you were there once upon a time,
But took it away with you when you left.

You say you can picture it now
With the clarity of a future recollection,
Seeing everything
As you will remember having seen it.
But when you arrive,
Each forgotten detail will jolt you
Like the missing step at the top of a dark stairway,
The vaguely felt logic of streets
Whose names you can never quite guess
Before you read them.

No doubt the temptation will be great
To imagine yourself inside small houses,
Stuck back from the road on a grassy slope
Or in a grove of shade trees.

You will wish then you had been born
To the life of a native,
Unedified by knowledge of return,
The fulfillment of departure.

As you ease into the driveway of your destination,
The lucid whiteness of dust
May occur to you as if for the first time—

How it hangs in the air
Like haze above a smoldering fire,
Never consumed, never the same.

Postcard from the Heartland

Stupidly, I crossed the Rockies at night,
made Denver by dawn, ate breakfast
and kept going. I got bleary-eyed about
mid-Kansas. The radio said it was 96.
I pulled onto the off ramp, finally,
delirious, thought: Instead of Zeus
missiles, why not an obelisk for Demeter,
at harvest farmers' daughters kneeling
in the raw to offer up sacred loaves?
In the Russell Diner, where I bought this
picture of wheat, I sat with truckers,
farm boys, old hands, sipped a Pepsi
and listened to crude one-liners passing
for wit. Loneliness is like a religion
here. I had a vision of your breasts,
bread of the angels, hard nipple rising
to my palm as you worked a brush through
your hair. Imagination's the devil.
I'd swear I saw the waitress transformed,
as she'd appear, smiling, to her lover.

Apart

Each night I find that star
we said was ours
and wonder what has brought me
to this: staring like a supplicant
at an ember of the universe
afraid it will suddenly go out.

Already the summer's half gone.
Each night my window's open,
the covers on my bed tossed back.
Every memory comes tinged
with regret, every thought:
crickets chirring the same slow rhythm
your breathing took on in sleep.

When I left I said you would always be with me.
I have a confession.

Each day I search the faces of women
for the look you carry in your eyes
like the torn half of a secret message.

And each day when the earth & sky
draw together like two eyelids,
I remember your touch
the way a blind man feeling the sun on his face
remembers light.

On My Own

All of a sudden a bare bright bulb
switched on in a dark room.
I must have been sleeping.
The same question repeated tirelessly,
What will you do? What will you do?
It seemed I'd lost my family,
a terrible accident.

What did they expect? I got a job.
I come home in the evenings
and stare at my books
lined up against the wall
like deserters.

If I think hard
phrases come back to me
like weird snippets of dreams:
ineluctable modality,
cognitive dissonance,
mythopoetic organicism.

I pick out the first book at hand,
The Psychopathology of Everyday Life,
and start to read,
chewing the sentences like peanut butter.
Several times and I figure it out.
I *knew* that.

I begin to worry I missed my calling.
What couldn't I do
with a scholar's free time?
Study the migratory habits of pencils,
learn to speak fluently
the language of beds.

Instead,
I find myself wrapped up in common sense,
repeating the simple lessons
over and over like a retarded child:
this is the world,
these are its people,
this is my life—

day and night unraveling a single thread
I know is secretly weaving
the suit of darkness
I'll be buried in.

Saying Good-bye to the Bureaucrats
At the Museum of Hopelessness

They are all here disguised as themselves
The ones without names
And the ones with titles embossed
On their smiles

The sanctimonious clerks
And shuffling janitors
The secretaries whose eyes reflect keyboards
Engraved with the letters
Of an indecipherable message

I walk by them looking for an exit

Past the man boxing his shadow
The woman who fell in love with one
And married the other

Past the child at a school desk
Wearing a television for a hat
The beetle in a glass jar
Dragging a ball of dung
Instead of rolling it

Shunted from office to office to fill out
The forms that will enable me to fill out
The forms till I arrive at the last door
Revolving of course
In an octagon of mirrors

Looking up the fluorescent corridor
I see their faces swollen like pumpkins
Peering from doorways

So this is the joke
I am the new acquisition
The man who wants out
Who walks around and around
In his little room of mirrors

But what they can't predict
Occurs like a shift in the wind

The stone I find in my shoe

When I lift it out
It splinters the light like a diamond

II

Dreaming Back

To Chandler

I.

Come home to an empty house,
I get undressed in my room
and stand by the window, looking out.
It's the first warm day of spring;
fools parade on the sidewalk.
Above them, unseen,
the skin of my belly sings.
I move into the light to mock them.
Crossing the hall to your room,
I stretch out on the rumpled sheets.
I lie still in your smell a long time,
trying to imagine moving inside you.

II.

Innocence was a kind of bravado.
I lounged on your bed and wrestled,
squeezing you by the wrists
when you came to chase me out.
You dropped my hands with a look
that spelled out my real name.
Worried about what you knew,
I beat you.
Beat you like my own dear conscience.
I know now I was wrong.
It was your own shame you suffered.

III.

You stumbled drunk from the car,
arm slung over the shoulder
of some jerk with my name.
What could I say,
collared by Jane's arm, a piece
of her ass squeezed in my hand?
I flinched from your big grin,
a con man stung by recognition.
At the dinner table I'd counter
your smirk with a quick glare.
The crisis always passed,
your curt insinuations
ignored by Mother, shunned by Dad.
When I think of all those nights
I lay wedged in a car's back seat,
trying to break loose. . . *Jesus.*

IV.

Secrecy without a secret.
But then, how could I have known?
She lay down in the shadow of a tree,
shrubbery all around,
the soft turf covered with dew.
I walk toward her, knees folding under,
enter dark water.
I always dreamed it would happen like this.

*

Except for the details:
groping with an unwieldy stick,
the urgent timing
of that last quick press in the wet grass.
The streetlamp has a halo of mist.
In its light, leaves are translucent,
an eerie moss green.
Sullen, estranged, I lie looking up at them.
Unmindful, she tells me her dream.
For three hours,
sitting on a knoll in back of the house,
I stare down the dark slope,
feeling the loss.
It was my only excuse.

V.

I have had to grow up.
The dreams?
Well, the dream is the same.
Sometimes I wake
and realize it was your face
that suddenly filled in.
The woman beside me sleeps.
I wonder if I am in her dreams,
they fool us so often.
We meet at last without dreams,
with an answer,
there where someone cries out,
O Mother, I am lost.

My Brother's Face

To Mark

Once upon a time, tells the Brahmana of
the hundred paths, gods and demons were at
strife. The demons said: "To whom can we
bring our offerings?" They set them all in
their own mouths. But the gods set the gifts
in one another's mouths. Then, Prajapati, the
primal spirit, gave himself to the gods.

—Martin Buber, *I and Thou*

I.

I loaf barefoot in the pond of shade
the maples spill over the lawn,
watch the sun glaring
through the woods' top branches,
strands of ground fog
twisting in the fields.

The screen door slaps
and before I can turn
you shout, "Catch!"

The football soars, a long, high spiral—

I sprint under as it spins down,
outstretched hands
closing around it like a nest
before I slip,
tumbling in a blur of sky and earth.

II.

You frown at the family portrait,
trying to see yourself
in the eyes of a boy
who must be you,
his face an embarrassing fact.
He grins eagerly, happy with his place,
staring out of the photograph
past you, his look so transparent
you feel exposed
and want to protect him.
You know everything he hasn't learned.
He knows everything you have forgotten.

In dreams sometimes he plays your part
while you watch from the air,
disembodied, invisible,
hearing your voice
speak words you haven't thought.
When you wake, he's as hard to picture
as your grandfather, who's dead.
You close your eyes, inhale,
and pretend you're covered with earth.
Your heart slows, hammer
pounding a nail deep—
your ballooned lungs lose count.
When your lips burst apart,
you gulp air like a beached survivor.

If you could see who you really are,
you wouldn't be afraid.
Your face is an impostor.
You hunt and hunt for yourself
in your eyelids' black mirror.

III.

Wrapped in the room's familiar dark,
you gaze at the ceiling's blurred screen,
a blizzard of lucent specks.
Your nerves quiver like a hummingbird's wings.
Pulse quickening, you think of that woman
so beautiful you can't envisage her face.
You shut your eyes and see her luminous body,
breasts smooth as new snow, her face
flashing in and out of focus,
changing into women you've seen
or made up, composites of perfect features.
You can't breathe deeply enough.
Your eyes sting, flooding.
You long to rise from your body
and explode to her touch like lit gas.

୬

Your eyes thrash under their lids,
tips of a wind-shook branch.

> *in a bare claret room you turn*
> *and she faces you like a mirror*
> *when you kiss a trap door drops*
> *you feel her body rising against yours*
> *as you both sink under*
> *an ache like a held breath*
> *a clenched throat*
> *mouth that can't hold out*
> *opening*
> *breathing water*

Startled awake,
you try to recall what you almost felt.
But your head's a heavy stone.
Sleep's black parachute blooms.

When your mind lights,
you have already landed.
You blink, bewildered to find yourself
in the same room, remembering only
a dream of rain.

IV.

What is the use of being a boy
if you are going to grow up
to be a man?

I'm writing to calm myself
because I woke, dreamless,
scared, my tongue a dry root.

If the wind had a fist
it would shatter glass.
Each time a gust rattles the window,
I start trembling and can't stop.
I feel December's full moon
tug at my bloodstream, my heart
racing like a cold engine.

I'm living out the banal dream of failure:
sitting at a desk, petrified,
unable to think. Time's almost up.
Reading the same question again and again,
I want to cry. It doesn't make sense.

༂

Imagining you, I was seeing myself.
I thought that what I remembered,
described, would reveal
what I want to tell you.

Instead, I feel like a child
wakened by dreams
who stands in the hallway
listening to the hush
of his parents' room.

V.

The wind has calmed to an icy breath,
shadows formed as when eyes
begin to see in the dark.
The path is dusted with snow,
the driveway drifted over in spots.
I walk down to the road and cross
to the low bank plows have scraped up.
Huddled in my coat,
I lift my boots in the slow two-step
people have always danced,
waiting in the cold.

From here the snow-sleek hill
sweeps down to woods,
its long, undulant slope jutting
into the lavender blur
of bare maple, beech and oak.

I watch mist lighten and shift
beyond Six Mile Creek.
When the high ridge looms,
my eyes feel like fists
unfolding.

Trudging up to the house,
I stop as though called
and look again: *Everywhere
form's silent asking.*

So much depends
upon

us
to answer, to witness.

VI.

Once I played dead
until you cupped my face
in your hands
and pleaded for me to live.
I heard you,
frightened by loneliness,
begging for your life.

Mark,
when you threw that pass
I outran myself
just to see your face
jubilant.

III

Wind and Strategy

All day the trees hunch their backs
like people waiting in the rain
to catch a bus.
Sparrows are only a guess.
Your eyes light on the vacant sill
or a quivering branch.
So you are tired of just looking out:
everywhere the dolor of metal boxes
on telephone poles,
a mothball fleet anchored in the sky.
Dozing off, you imagine
the Sea of Loneliness on the moon
or the hands of old women
lowering shades at dusk
in Grand View, Kansas.
You wake in late afternoon
to find the buildings across the street
obscured by mist, their windows black
except for one amber light
glowing in the den of a retired clerk.
You peer closer as he examines
a rare stamp through his quizzing glass:
an etching of this city,
skyscrapers surrounded by apartment flats,
block after block emerging from fog
until he locates his own window,
and through it, as you are seeing now,
the lamp above his desk,
the book of stamps, but nowhere,
no matter how tightly he squints, himself.
Though you know it's impossible,
when he looks up and stares out the window,
you have the feeling your eyes have met.

The Tie That, Binding, Liberates

For Thomas Johnson

Curled in the overstuffed wing chair,
my wife muffles a yawn as she scans
the local weekly one more time.
I put down my book and unwrap
this thin, mysterious cigar
a friend gave me last night.
Rough-surfaced, coffee-bean brown,
it looks like a twig, was hand-rolled
in Brazil he said. I light it—
and light up, savor good tobacco
with a suspicion of some spice
whose name remains elusive as its tinge.
Grinning between puffs, I consider
how the urge to share becomes,
for some of us, recreation, our delight
sent forth to multiply and replenish
the earth with the fruitfulness
of metaphor's original sin:
that copulative, promiscuous *is*.
The big black ant that's been
wandering around for days
scurries from under the sofa; rather,
bumbles, its legs not quite as long
as the carpethairs. See what I mean?
Through the smoke of my friend's
magical cigar, the ant bouncing
patiently toward the kitchen becomes
a prairie schooner, lost but headed
west on the trackless plains of Nebraska.

Houseplants

For their unceasing prayer
We reverence them
Like the relics of saints

Rooted in earth
They commune with Paradise

They make of our windows
Fenestellas
To which we bring
Offerings of water

Receiving their benediction
In the wordless language
Of rapture

        Verdant tongues
Stretched to take
The sun's wafer of light

The Life of Weeds

Along the house
jupiter's-beards nod like drunks
on their lean stalks,
whispering to themselves,
mañana, mañana.
In the morning their leaves flush
and stretch out flat in the sun,
each cell a delicate gem.
The claret blossoms
shake a thousand tiny bells,
and bees come with the folded hands of priests,
chanting hymns.

Strawberry

Roughly heart-shaped lump
of luscious, blood-red pulp
embedded with hundreds
of minute seeds, couriers
trained to deliver the secret
formula of replication
in code that only
warm, moist dirt can crack.

Candy's precursor,
pendulous drop
of fragrant sweetness
no beak or mouth
could ever resist:
crow or deer, nourished,
becomes sower, the plant's
unwitting accomplice.

&

Six quarts of strawberries
luxuriantly heaped
in a cream-white
porcelain bowl.

I pick one out and hold it up:

What I want to know is
who
thought of this?

Eating a Peach

1.

Pick one just beginning
to go soft and hold it
at arm's length. Imagine
such a planet against
the backdrop of outer space.
On its surface pastel gases
swirl and mix the exquisite
palette of a tropical sunset.

2.

An old pomologist going blind,
fit the peach gently
to your palm; close your hand.
Two fingers will caress
the pubescent skin while
your pious thumb contemplates
the sealed orifice.

3.

A connoisseur of fruit,
lift it to your nose:
savor the subtle bouquet
of this ingeniously
bottled nectar.

4.

At last:
get a firm, reverent grip and
sink your teeth.

This is not for the prim.
Your greedy tongue
will try to get every drop
that slides out of reach.

Too soon you'll be down
to the last scarlet-edged bit,
the sweetest.
But when the flavor's gone
there's still reminiscence.

Hold the seed on your tongue,
a tiny petrified brain
with a single thought,
eternal, platonic: *Peach.*

Another Portrait of the Artist

After Louis Malle and Polly Platt's *Pretty Baby*

I.

Night after night Bellocq stands near the bar,
nursing a bourbon, rapt in the sensuousness
of merely looking. His blue linen sports coat
also sets him apart; naval officers wear
dress whites; the others, dark formal suits,
befitting their wealth and this,
''the best damn bawdy house in New Orleans.''
The low women, coiffed, perfumed,
and decked out in high fashion,
adorn the parlor's plush decor
like debutantes, stepping out
to greet the gents with gracile,
fawning caresses and playful leers.
The johns love the whole routine,
from the first flattering lie
to the last moan crooned just before they come.
Bellocq won't buy their illusion.
But then, they disregard his art.
While they flush and strut upstairs,
he watches the flowing ritual dance
like some skid row evangelist turned saint,
his fanatic eyes joyfully vigilant.

II.

"Why would anybody want to take a picture
of a piece of ass?" —Hattie's fancyman,
hung over, barefoot and still in shorts,
leans on the camera. Bellocq shoves him off,
takes account of Hattie's smoldering look
as dispassionately as he reads the light.
Wearing a sheer, disheveled nightgown, hair mussed,
she sits back, queenly in a rattan wing chair,
deciding to postpone anger.
Unable to get his Havana lit, the brute
tosses it aside; looking at her, squints.
"Where'd the hell you get those earrings?"
"Why, you give 'um to me last night!
Don'tcha remember?" He lumbers toward her.
"*Christ*, woman, those are *real* emeralds. Now,
why would I give *real* emeralds to a whore?"
Bellocq squeezes off the shot a split-second
before he lunges into the picture, precisely
when Hattie's eyes see what's what, and blaze.

When Bellocq brings the photograph to Hattie,
the other girls surround him, lured
by his refusal to let them look. In the melee
Violet grabs it, sees her mother trans-
formed: "She's . . . so . . . pretty." Looking
over her shoulder, Fanny, stunned, chimes in:
"Christ be! She looks like an angel."

III.

Where but in a high-class brothel
could Bellocq have found women
who sported bare flesh as casually
as nymphs? Who dressed up to undress,
their social graces lavish foreplay,
distinguished by that honesty
from drawing room artifice.

The whores take to calling him *Papa*,
because he treats them like
daughters who've reached the age
when a good father's afraid
to take them on his lap.
Though they make teasing assaults
on his quixotic decorum,
push tits *décolleté* against his chest,
confound him with an octopus of hands
that stroke and pinch, he never
returns other than paternal embrace or
photographer's brief, dictatorial clasp,
could no more escort one of them upstairs
than could the house piano player, a black.

But nightly, watching his girls
entertain clients, Bellocq looks
like one of the blessed. His ardor—
the self-enjoyings of self-denial,
the moment of desire prolonged,
heightened into trance—becomes
adoration's sacrificial fire.

He falls into art as into self,
greedy, with meticulous, cold intent
manipulates model, pose and light
to own the beauty his vision
half creates. His only absolution
is success. An artist ends
where he began, becomes
what he desired to possess.
We might well say, "This is Bellocq,"
as we stare again at a photograph
of a woman whose beauty alarms us.

The Noble in Exile

In memory of Bert Meyers

1.

Behind the wheel of his car
he knows the shame of a dog
forced to wear clothes.

Brake lights flash on
like targets in a pinball game.

A tail pipe farts smoke
like a machine gun.

He wants to get out
and go on by foot alone,
nothing in his pockets
but his briar, tobacco,
matches and a spoon.

2.

He watches gulls flap above the bay,
handkerchiefs waving good-bye
from the decks of an invisible ship.

If he had his way, beggars would ride,
imagination become, for the good,
a magic wand,

able to change a pebble
squeezed by a destitute hand
into a gem,

weapons into relics locked up
in some museum,

ads into mystical poems
a child could understand.

3.

From an ancient line of peasants,
he needs few words,

whose forebear,
when that king demanded pie,
gathered blackbirds.

Dusk

The low sun dissolves
Spreading a stain of ripe mango
Between plum-colored clouds

In treetops the elves watch
Piping a tune on the flute of forgetfulness

Like a last thought before sleep

A dove homes toward the glowing rim
Dragging a blue sheet
That turns black
When no one is looking

After Hearing Roethke Read

The self persists like a dying star.

Now the record has stopped,
The echo chamber far back in the brain
Holds the silence
Like a raised, benedictory hand.

Outside, the air is cool and drenched
With the scent of lilacs.
The full moon still cradles
The frail silhouette of her unborn child,
And the wren the cat set down
By the porch still gives tongue
To its dark song.

Nothing has changed.
But even the stars seem renewed,
The offerings of some accepted
Long after they burned themselves out.

Disrobing the Body of Thought

The cat ambles over, her swollen nipples
Swaying in the grass.
She nudges my leg
And turns to stare into darkness.

She is more cunning than anything out there.
Her body remembers perfectly
The blindness of mice,
The clumsiness of dogs,
The hunger for affection
Of the hand that feeds her.

She will die,
Caught in the blades of the fan
When the car starts up as she naps.

Alone now, she stalks a long breath
That swells near the ground,
Prophecy of an ancient dream
Fulfilling itself in moonlight and wind,
The damp earth odors of evening.

Something stirs and the fur bristles along her spine.
Just like that. Again,
Nothing.

Late Spring Night,
Driving Home with Friends

For Ray Carver

Direction dissolves
in the float of the headlights
as the car unwinds the road
up a low mountain.

Inside my belly
tall strands of barley
are swaying in a warm breeze.

From the back-seat window
I watch the mist
sifting like sediment
around the moon.
The car downshifts,
climbs into fog.

Eyes shut,
I let the backwash of blackness take me,
smiling to think
I could have valued my own life
so much.

Conversation with the Inner Man

For Charles Simic

> *Though you utter*
> *Every one of my words,*
> *You are a stranger.*
> *It's time you spoke.*

One humid June night
the late ride home
became a languorous cruise
on the quick-dipping,
slowly curving back road—
a dream I wished would go on and on
ended in the carport:
I watched my hand turn the key,
switch off the headlights,
and sat for a moment
a little bit scared,
wondering if it's dangerous
to let him drive.

Walking the flagstone path
to the house,
I felt him freeze,
stopped. What
this time?

The sky moonless
oceanic black, stars
glimmering like the lanterns
of deep-sea fish.

All around,
millions of leaves
breathing.

Spooked, I wanted to walk
whistling to the porch,

but he balked, flexed senses
easing only when my nostrils
caught the fragrance
of wet, mown grass—

tang of a memory from way back,

his joy
womb speech,
heart talk.

The Mesmerist's Pearl

Thoughts drifting skyward snag on the full moon.
I lose myself and find myself blessed,
Time's flowing felt as stream around a stone.

A little girl who wonders why dark's grown
So light finds out: eyes seduced, her undressed
Thoughts drifting skyward snag on the full moon.

Between locked doors a watchman thinks *soon;*
Gazing, envisions his wife's swollen breasts,
Time's flowing felt as stream around a stone.

A trucker driving a long stretch alone
Laughs till tears come, glows as effervesced
Thoughts drifting skyward snag on the full moon.

Slouched in a car, a woman, sixteen, croons
Her love to sleep, his head in her lap's nest,
Time's flowing felt as stream around a stone.

The song's his dream, a slow, improvised tune.
She ad-libs lyrics, just hums when caressed
Thoughts drifting skyward snag on the full moon,
Time's flowing felt as stream around a stone.

For a Child Dreaming

Poor child wrapped now
in sleep's cocoon,
tonight
you are the moon's
marionette.
But there'll be
no flight
tomorrow
when you wake up.
In school
your thoughts
will stray (butterfly
in a field
of Queen Anne's lace)
until your teacher
calls the name
that's tied to you
for life.

Blinking and Breathing

Cora, our sleek calico,
lifts head off paws
and shows me all her teeth,
uncurled tongue
the petal of a lotus.

Too languid to read any more,
I shift in the recliner,
put cheek to fist
like a saboteur laying an ear to track,
half listen for tire-whirr
on blacktop, an engine's rapid fire
strafing the zeppelins of thought.

A car without a muffler guns past.
Peeved, I follow its diminishing wake
mapless on back roads, at last
turn down a murky lane,
exhausted, lost.

The cat tugs at my pantleg.
Recoiling from light,
my mind staggers back,
unable to remember money spent,
thumbing an empty wallet.

Jaws pulled open, my whole body shudders
as though in death throes dying to speak,
at the final moment smiling,
forgetting what it was
that couldn't wait.

April Night, Turning In

I switch off the lamp,
and instantly
my thoughts abscond.

Entranced, I stare until
I see the hanging fern
silhouetted against
the window:

fountain of ladders
sunlight will climb,
rejoicing another day.

When I slip into bed,
my body stretches
beside yours, glowing,
settles down,
a seed tucked into loam.

My mind, that dark cloud,
grows heavier, lets fall,
finally, a soft rain.

Navigation Self-Taught

The current swirls around my neck
as I tilt and flop,
swept along like an empty paper cup.

Near shore, two tour boats pass.
People stare, afraid to look.
A child points. I yell.

An old couple shake their heads
and blush. A man leans over
and explains there isn't any room.

Stunned, I think of a log,
and just then one bobs near.
I haul up and lie on top.

My feet churn like forks beating eggs.
My cupped hands dive and pull
steady as paddlewheels.

Rounding the bend to the river's mouth,
I surge past. Everyone cheers.
I wave. The boats circle upstream.

Kneeling on the beach, breathless,
I look up at the ocean.
My heart bolts like a fish thrown back.

Ringed above the horizon
are seven red suns.
The sky glows coral everywhere I turn.

The Lost Body of Childhood

For Norman O. Brown

What the ears want most
is to drop off the head like ripe fruit
and lie on a beach among shells
echoing music by favorite composers
with intermissions
silent as a drawn bow.

The eyes too dream of escape.
They long to flutter their lashes
like butterflies shedding cocoons
wander from panorama to prospect
seeing everything like children
for the first time.
When they grew old
they'd retire to a peak in the Himalayas
overlooking a valley and a lake
envisioned now when they close
bored to tears by the geography of walls.

Petit bourgeois
the tongue and palate are pretty much content
two old partners with steady business.
Evenings they sit back of the shop
discussing what would be the tastiest meal
neither agreeing nor objecting
but merely offering up
successive morsels for thought
as they smoke and drink beer
in shared wistfulness.

The nose is an enigma
a Chinese butler
always there
aloof as he is dependable.
Who can tell what he secretly desires?
One can only guess
from his passion for arranging flowers
the way he lingers over a cluster of lilac
or a sprig of jasmine.

Genitals are the royalty of flesh.
The penis a courtly monarch
leaps up at the barest thought.
Vagina the queen wears a purple cape
adorned with a single priceless pearl.
They are suited perfectly to each other.
Desire is their magic lamp.
Each night millions kneel in obeisance.

There is a sixth sense
perceived through the others
existing before them
a presence like air.
And yet a person who takes off his face
in the privacy of his own mind
may gasp like an asthmatic
terrified.
He will return to his senses
if he returns
like the newborn
every nerve blossoming.

A Note on the Author

David Dayton lives just outside Ithaca, New York, where he is employed part-time as a typesetter for *The Cornell Daily Sun*. His wife Nancy Cavallaro is working toward a doctorate in soil chemistry at Cornell.

He edits and publishes *Alembic: A Magazine of Poetry.* This book is his first.

Colophon

The author designed this book and set the type on a Compugraphic phototypesetter. Titles are set in 14 point Goudy Bold; the poems, in 10 point Trump Medieval with three points of leading. Glad Day Press of Ithaca, New York, printed a first edition of 500 copies in June 1979.

Publication of this book was made possible by a grant from the National Endowment for the Arts, a federal agency.